Praise for
Reverberating Voices

Reverberating Voices is a sacred passageway to another world where justice, truth, and beauty intersect to reimagine a better pathway. Calling upon ancestral voices, collective wisdom, and genealogies of resistance, Garay summons a generation of warriors, culture keepers, and relatives who spin a kinship matrix from Nicaragua to revolution, from politics to love, from ceremony to landscapes. This powerful new collection will teach us about thrivance and how we can all get there together---to a place of radical love. A must read for anyone serious about love and transformative justice!

> **–Andrew Jolivette**, Professor and Chair, Department of Ethnic Studies,
> University of California, San Diego and Author of
> *Research Justice: Methodologies for Social Change*

The poetry of Ernesto M. Garay is what happens when the seemingly unstoppable forces of racism, xenophobia, and the general heartlessness of capitalism come up against will and determination of a quiet immovable dignity. Early on the poet Garay tells the reader that this work emerges from the fringes of broken history. The poet then spends the rest of the book making them whole. Garay's *Reverberating Voices* is filled with understated anthems woven together by a steady craft that leads the reader by way of detail, humor, an unflinching honesty and an expansive soul through the landscape of a hostile country. When times call for strength and courage read this stunning collection and allow these voices to reverberate in the depths of your spirit for years to come.

> **–Matt Sedillo**, Author of *City On The Second Floor* and *Mowing Leaves Of Grass*

Ernesto M. Garay's poetry is a complex psychic possession moving back and forth between valence spirits and the music of local gestures almost painted still; painted history with multi-intelligences. These poems lead your mind to new potentials of psychic cohabitation; your kinetic place or ability to listen as ancestor, informal witness, revolutionary protagonist, and poetry fan all at once. Reverberating Voices is the volcanic dance of a healer; the ceremony in the alley; the wisdom of our oldest friends.

> **–Tongo Eisen-Martin**, San Francisco's 8th Poet Laureate

Reverberating Voices

FLOWERSONG
PRESS

by
Ernesto M. Garay

FLOWERSONG
PRESS

FlowerSong Press
Copyright © 2022 by Ernesto M. Garay
ISBN: 978-1-953447-61-6
Library of Congress Control Number: 2022948685

Published by FlowerSong Press
in the United States of America.
www.flowersongpress.com

Cover Images by Amanda Ayala
Cover Design by Priscilla Celina Suarez
Set in Adobe Garamond Pro

NOTICE: SCHOOLS AND BUSINESSES
FlowerSong Press offers copies of this book at quantity discount with bulk
purchase for educational, business, or sales promotional use. For information,
please email the Publisher at info@flowersongpress.com.

CONTENTS

Outlawed

Looking for a Reflection

Deafening Voices

Healing Fault Lines

Border Crossings

The Reverberating Voices

Today I write my reverberating story,
a thudding voice buried deep into the sea of the abyss, resuscitating
the unconscious voices, heaving from my tired mouth,

> dust stuck to lips that open like blood scabs,
> at the fringes of broken history,
> I can't throw my songs away; first sounds are not lost to memory.

> Not all the words written on the empty pages,
> could soak up the tears
> you feel for your lost migrant children,

> Not a peach or plum as innocent and lively,
> as the pulsations of their red hearts,
> you wonder if your children still dream.

But today, I write my reverberating story,
my heart longs for lingering healing, recording these words on
to the empty white pages, believing that dreams are the language of our ancestors.

> I must remember because they're ready to dismember
> I must remember because they're ready to dismember
> I must remember because they're ready to dismember

> My humanity, history, dignity, and voice
> My humanity, history, dignity, and voice
> My humanity, history, dignity, and voice

> I write my feelings close to my heart
> I write my feelings close to my heart
> I write my feelings close to my heart

> Today I write my reverberating story,
loosening the wings from my words and letting them fly freely,
multiplying into a thousand voices, finding myself in them.

Crossing Dreamer

I want to live in the United States, among the American
Dreamers, the Green-tailed Hummingbird, gentle rain
drops on the roof in the springtime, not among the
garbage dumps, the inflated dollar, and devalued peso.
Not even in the windowless house where I live along
with the plant where we work like the savage black
mule. I dream out loud, and I sing to you: José José's
bolero: "Amar y Querer" until my heart bursts, and
the yellow and speckled stars appear tonight. And I strap
on my white Nikes and cross myself. Before I cross over
to the other side of the grated fence, I finish this poem
written to you. In my fluttering heart, I see your glistening
eyes and turn into a Lioness. There's no turning back to
                    where I have no name!

Oh, Beautiful Monarch Butterfly

1

I dream deeply with the Monarch Butterfly
as the vision comes to me oh so vividly:
florescent-orange and black, it soars,
sputters and flutters against the wind.
I examine its true colors, visioning how a
butterfly is born. I get distracted by the brown-
soil dirt as the Redwood trees grounded so
sincerely, and their shallow roots withstand wind.
The wind rustles
the green leaves as the wind blows and blows.
Then it comes to me like an idea that comes
to the deep thinker that examines it like a
feast for the senses: The Monarch Butterfly
begins as a caterpillar, creeping through the
moist dirt as the sun feeds it with radiant power.

2

Then it goes into a chrysalis, converting into
a pearl: The Monarch Butterfly sputters and sputters
in front of my wide-opened eyes. It awes me with
beauty that comes from ashes—some say!

I am fallen upon by the curtain of the boundless sky.
I greet the butterfly that didn't pour from the earth's roof.
This creature, a borderless Butterfly, fluidly flying:
feminine in nature and can fly over any barrier.

A springtime soul lingers between flowers and borders,
sowing seeds of peace for the global world.
Queen butterfly, she's without walls, without guards,
resituates herself on top of the milkweed, nourishing
her flight with visibility, existence, and light.

3

Monarch butterflies in a swarm can move mountains.
They are our physical ancestry: human, animal, reptile,
shellfish plants as well as the human consciousness.
They frame all the raw material from gyration into stars,
Then planets and solar systems—in full flight shaking, Earth.
Two butterflies make love in front of my eyes, sparking a
memory of spirits of deceased ancestors who mysteriously
reappear at the same time in the Central Hills of Mexico:
butterflies flutter in an endless stream into a few Oyamel
fir trees where they take roost and sleep so deeply.

Facing Your Borders

There is the US-Mexican Border, the chain-linked fence, topped with barbwire,
a monolithic apparatus, extending its tentacles and piercing claws.

The Border on the threshold of   1,952 miles, a homogenous monster
living in a desert where the rain burns deeper than molten lava.

It closes in the broken and unopen sky. It aligns with voices.
And ghosts thicker than any human skin among the skeletons
in the desert.

On the Northern side of the Border, there's a TV in every house.
And people lounge as wounds open in their hearts like fractures
on frozen white ice.

Here mental borders slumber in the collective psyche, and there's solitude
in each body. People will cross-cultural spaces, holding up their arms,
protecting themselves from ghostly   illegals or Communists.

And some protecting their prized possessions while some drown in
their ignorance, not seeing through their broken window.
They are not seeing or hearing that a few people in the world have
all the money.

But this history, a reminder of why the US-Mexican Border has stood for
security and democracy and whose blood spills on to streets on both
sides of the border.

You can't kill ideals. I am dangerous. Defined in opposition to you'll,
but I walk as I am.
I am vitamins for the future,
my ideas will flourish tomorrow,
today, I spread my roots, and spirit sees me,
I will not sell out to your borders in the face of death,
and that is shouting something huge, so huge,
                                        shakes me.

But more than fear, is my Amor for justice
more than my ego is to move aside,
when someone talks about the fact. But today,
only a few speak the truth, yesterday no
one spoke the truth,

none came to my side to say I was right, because
I was isolated, broke, without community.
So today, I face your physical and mental borders, I stand erect,
I speak up and align with others
who see my mirror of truth.

This is writhe, pain, anxiety, and loneliness,
but also, power, trust, love, it gifts a human with those
mystical qualities of the Spirit that humanizes the human,
a gift to us, what is missing,
most vibrant and full of utmost beauty and force, as I face
your borders.

The Relentless Farmworker

In 1951, Rafael Morales, the relentless
farmworker, rides the roaring gray bus
from Oaxaca, Mexico on his way to Sonoma
County, California; the exhaust's black smoke
spits into her night sky. The clitter/clatter
of the worn-out tires outside and the chit/chat
inside knock together. Morales' brown eyes
are wide open like an aperture or shutter of a
camera, blinking and blinking, and focusing on his
past as fragmented and flashes of American
history. Rafael Morales, the relentless farmworker
deported from the US--24-to-25--times back to his
bounded home country: Tequixtepec, Mexico,
lost as the horseshoe on the Westerner's map.
When he crosses over and arrives in Sonoma
County, two months later, this time around on a
sunny Sunday morning, the sun shines on him as it shatters
his dark side. Under the magic beneath this unveiled
the sun, Rafael Morales, the relentless farmworker
during mass prays to God to find another job.
Seeing the Chevy light blue truck outside,
 on board three-to-four braceros, one of them
 smiles with sheer delight split ear-to-ear. He tells
 Rafael like a messenger from above that he has
 the job. And off he goes with them with a meager
50 cents, hardly making a sound in his deep
pockets. Rafael Morales, the relentless farmworker,
is on his way to Santa Rosa to the Grace Brother's
Ranch--where he will pick golden prunes and the
White unicorn roams freely. History pushes its
way to the present. Harold McClish, his boss--
compassionate like an overflowing reservoir--
helps him attain the miraculous green card.
Rafael Morales, the relentless farmworker, now
as *legal* as the American in US history, primed
            for the American Dream.

The Full Moon

The Full Moon's energy inspires the Pacific Ocean's water currents
to flow in several directions like the wind that blows

on the four corners of the earth. Its periodic light   peers through the leaves
and wind blows towards low pressure, and air rises in the atmosphere where
they meet. Deep roots:

the tree intertwined into the soil: grounded into the Mother Earth's ombligo.
The umbilical cord is buried to mark the birth
                         of a child.

A yellow moth wavers frantically under the moon and wings speckled with
golden dots.

Merry mystic man whispers into the sorcerer's ear:
he mentions to her that this luminous light, reflects the energy

of a dream and the moth, an ally, and a spirit are a message to
awaken to the light: the wondrous effulgence beams on the ocean.

The moon's star-crossed and spiritual might exerts its force on the white sparrow.

While it catches flight, one yellow star or two besides its brightness,
the full moon, a satellite of life, beautifies the mysterious sky.

We are connected
to the splendid light.

Lost in the Desert

We get desperate as the fierce Sonora Desert sears as it somewhere

hides the wells and becomes withered trees in its heart.
Our water supply, drying—

Now, our bottles are history, and twelve Salvadoran compatriots died
and were lost forever:

They were swallowed up by the fierce heat, despite their efforts.

We have become desperate and drunk our deodorants, perfumes,
and urine like orangutans.
Abandoned in the desert by our Coyote,

listen!   *eight of us lost as sheep*
                             eight of us lost as dogs

for two days as the fluttering feasting birds fly above,

waiting for us to become prey.

We say our prayers,
pray to the highest power
and apply toothpaste and makeup
to our sunburned faces.

We hope for a miracle as a twig that bears flowers.

I continue to stagger like a fallen pug, beaten.
But as my eyes partly close and sight becomes a mist,
my heart pounds against my chest, and my spirit is rekindled.
I see the Jeep approaching and hear someone cry behind
me: *We are blessed! We are blessed! We are blessed!*

Betrayal

Kike feels giddy
as the eight-year-
old boy who opens
his presents on Christmas Eve.

> He slept like a baby, serenely,
> to the sound of the warm
> wind. Kike's hometown--Sonsonate,
> a department of El Salvador, remains
> the heart of the Pipil culture, the pulse
> of ancient Mayan traditions: where
> the few speakers of the Nahuatl language live.
> Sonsonate's sun is free of morning clouds.

The Toucan birds sing melodiously
while they talk to each other.
But Kike sees the warning sign
of the Salvadoran Death-Squad:
the painted White-Hand, imprinted
on the center of his front-blue door,
a warning that el *comunista*
will soon be disappeared somewhere
into the abyss while the night sky is eternal.

> His stomach is nauseous, tight as rope.
> He's black-listed and pushed to invisibility,
> like Jesus, who was condemned to death by Pontius Pilate.
> Kike feels the cut of the sharp knife,
> cutting deep into his bones.
> Kike is not involved in subversive activities.

So, he could escape death and torture!
Yet he now needs to flee like fish
that escape from whales or sharks.
So he could escape death and torture.
Tomorrow his journey will begin:
He will try to cross the US-Mexican border.

I only Look Illegal

see the cracked mirror
    fall from the blue sky
on my shadow and
    shatter to the ground
        can't look in the mirror:
    invisible like the invisible man

i only look illegal

        i pick up the scattered
           shards and glue them
    to the black wall i look
      into the sea of mirrors and see
    nobody i glue more
        fragments of the mirror-
like the lunatic from the
      full moon on my white wall

i only look illegal

but thinking that i am
alone as the last leaf
the cracked mirror not forgotten
that descended from the sky

la Frontera, rooted in my mind
jarred out of emotional ambivalence

I only look illegal

My Red Dress

My body is for sale, sinning out of necessity.
A prostitute: I need to beckon men from my window.
Ready to wear my red dress like spilling red paint.
I will splash out from the window into men's eyes.

A prostitute: I need to beckon men from my window.
El coyote took all my money and purse, victimized.
I will splash out from my window into men's eyes.
Stranded in Tijuana, want to earn money to cross over.

El Coyote took all my money and purse, abandoned.
Luis, my husband, migrated to San Francisco; I love him.
Stranded in Tijuana, want to earn money to cross over.
Like me, he fled the Nicaraguan Revolution, needing refuge.

Luis, my husband, migrated to San Francisco; I love him.
He's my plant of the most tender kind, born of the wet night.
Like me, he fled the Nicaraguan Revolution, needing refuge.
Luis, I miss you like the sky misses the stars and flowers miss the rain.

He's my plant of the most tender kind, born of the wet night.
My heart bleeds pain as hurt erupts in every place in my body.
Luis, I miss you like the sky misses the stars and flowers miss the rain.
One day I will see you again and birth your child.

My heart bleeds pain as hurt erupts every place in my body.
I am stripped away from my country, singing a song of longing and separation.
One day I will see you again and birth your child.
I yearn for a home like a lost nomad with no earth to stand on.

I am stripped away from my country, singing a song of longing and separation.
I need to put on my red dress to work from my window.
I yearn for a home like a lost nomad with no earth to stand on.
Have no choice but to lure men, my lottery ticket, out of here!

The Ticket to America

This is the afternoon when the wind carries sea salt, aromatic blooms, and Scrub Oak leaves as we arrive in Oceanside, San Diego.

This is the day when the ocean breeze floats above the tops of the cresting waves of the ocean.
This is the day when it's exciting enough that memory lit my mind like a spotlight, knowing that I might meet my cuzin.

A long drive, we drive on the 101 in the green Plymouth Duster. Pops and I are tired. Swarms of gnats. The ever-moving scattered clouds above and the unknown stories are ready to unravel quickly over the next three hours and see if we can trust the so-called coyote.

The olive-green JanSport duffle bag that I grasp like a Loomis Security Guard. The cream-white Los Angeles Dodgers Jersey lies in the bag, wondering if it would fend off INS detection, and on top of the securely stacked: $3000.

The look of legality and a US citizen: The use of the Dodgers Jersey, providing cuzin Julio the cultural markers to pass as American? The safety of Julio is like a tortoise under its shell. The way back to El Salvador is not safe, and deportation is cruel and harsh as rocks in the mountain.

How each day, we'd speak with Julio on the phone. How each day, we'd shared prayers for his safe crossing across the Frontera. You'd say dangerous so pray. I'd say the sun shines tomorrow, and white doves fly.

How always, Pops has a plan and hatred for Dodger's blue.

And the gray pavement hurts under us. Flashing flickering, beaming headlights become brighter: the white 58 Chevy truck pulls into the Days Inn parking lot. How the air strained, grew dry.

By the time we reached the blue-eyed man, I'd know that Pops is a sage, but the Dodger's jersey: the ticket to America?

Seeing Me

Seeing the soldado's eyes,
I eye his guarded fear.
He looks like a knotted tie,
like ready to make robotic commands
like he needs to gush himself on me

                   peering

with his eyes, he penetrates into my mind
and asks for my *papeles*

I feel my heart
it is thumping

it's small

        as a grackle
        it is as

            vibrant
            and

            that
            is

            good

Kind a so
I reach into my pockets for my *carné*

And I think of something about
home

Something true
(maybe about wanting to scream for sure)

That just happened to spurt
out of my mind

When I see his eyes,
sirens cry out

I need to slow down
I need to see the womb

In my bonified eyes
with my

       tongue

    on

        fi

          re
and

  it

    is not
holding

back any

     more:

Please let me cruzar
la Frontera!

Please let me cross over to *los estados*!

I shout

Seeing my eyes,

he sees me

      and says he has a job to do

         and walks away

        ¡A hora si! it is time to

       cross

War on Earth

1524

Quetzaltenango

The poet would speak of
Pedro De Alvarado and his henchmen,
who came with spoiled seeds:
like barbarians to perpetuate
fear.

He tells how the Spanish Conquistadores slaughtered the Mesoamericans.
Guatemala was a countryside
turned butcher shop.

Captain Tecum Umán, who launched himself in the air and flew
with his plume feathers, birthed
on his body.

He flew over De Alvarado and, with the force
of the mother water, snakes,
stars, and lakes, and all—
struck the head of the horse with his silver sword.

Pedro De Alvarado's horse's head was torn off and divided into two.
The conquistador released himself from the decapitated horse.

And he bounced back on his feet. Again, Captain Umán catapulted into the sky
to fly high like lightning. When he descended, Alvarado eluded him.

Then he punctures Tecum with his sword. Tecum Umán and Alvarado's
sword became one: the taker of his life.
The dogs went to maul Captain Umán.

Alvarado contemplated the vanquished: Quetzal split open, his plumes
sprouted on his arms and legs, his wings torn, the triple
crown of pearls and diamonds.

He called his soldiers. Alvarado asked:
"Look!" he obligated them to take off their helmets.

The kids were seated in circle
with the poet. One of them asked: "And you saw all
this? Have you seen it? You heard it"
"Yes," he replied.
"You were there?"—asked the kids.

"No. The ones that were here, none of ours' survived!"
The poet would point toward the movement
of clouds and the light that penetrated
the canopy of the trees.

"Will the swords come?"—they asked— "Will the feet of the horse gallop?"
"The rain of arrows? The smoke?" "Listen,"--
he would say, "and direct your ears
to the ground filled with stampedes."

And he would point to and smell
the history in the wind, touching
it on the polished rocks by the river
and recognize the taste munching on
specific herbs, like,

without hurry, like,

he who munches on sadness.

Nicaragua

In Nicaragua, my father's home country, crickets
sing, and iguanas swell. By now, feeling waves
roll beneath my feet, pulling me through the
dilatory nights of the war. In Managua, pops and
moms take me where the children's sun and the
song is taken away and freedom and stomachs
are empty.
I pace myself behind pops and moms, walking
towards the little boy with the bloated belly
and an unstitched baseball in hand. Moms
puts $20 in his grasp. Humbly he says gracias!
Then he runs away. Pops says I'm lucky,
being born in the US.

The Virus in San Francisco

Please! Booming hangover, go away! I am lost in my headache as it pounds my brain, displaced in my body, and in pain. Insane I have become, becoming a heavy drinker, sucking up the Brass Monkey and one shot of Jägermeister.

Partying in the Studio West parking lot last night—hanging out and having fun with Doug and Ricky in San Francisco, past two in the morning as God laughs from above with scorn.

I dropped two Tylenols to inspire the blood to flow into my head, hoping that the pain would go away into the distant past. I want to face my demons: eye-to-eye.

I dropped two Tylenols an attempt to inspire the blood to flow into my head, hoping that the pain would go away into the distant past. I want to face my demons: eye-to-eye.

With the red Safeway punch-in employee card in hand like the Visa Card, I slide it straight across the punch-in box: Beep!

It beeps like the smoke detector that sounds off at mom's house as she makes those mouth-watering *pupusas* for us to eat.

My stomach gurgles, not once, not twice, but three times. I want to eat. I want to munch on that tortilla with melted queso--puya!

While wars waged in Central America and the U.S., many flee, and blood spills over and across the US-Mexican border. I am battling AIDS because Joey, my Store Manage is working today.

The story has it that he has the AIDS virus: that weird and strange illness, inspiring rain death.

It's an attack from hell: white, Latino, and black gay men in Frisco are dropping like flies. Why? I don't know! All I know is that he has it.

And Joey's voice thunder strikes me. Hello, he says. Hello, I reply, as my heart is a maze of desires.

Joey is just as human as me. His enlivened smile, unthreatening and loving as a fragile flower, opened to the warmth of spring.

I greet him with my straight-full smile and politely say hi! Hoping he didn't offer to shake my hand; he's so close that I could feel his blue eyes.

The day I found out about his reddish-pink pock-a-dots—scattered scars on both of his arms, signaling: AIDS, some say; fear of imminent death had begun to stab at my mind and thoughts. It's hard to face Joey.

The automatic doors split wide open in front of my blinking eyes; I walk out like an ant escaping the rain to the Diamonds Heights Safeway parking lot to gather the Safeway carts.

The AIDS virus! How am I going to avoid Joey all day? I must hide, but the supply closet is not a comfortable place to escape. So why is death on my shoulders and following me around? The clock ticks and ticks!

I pray to Jesus that I don't have the VIRUS. My story reminds me that the VIRUS reflects the dark clouds one encounters in one of those Stephen King sci-fi novels.

The one that highlights the VIRUS outbreak somewhere in the U.S. What's the title of that novel? It outlines the release of a strain of influenza modified for biological warfare.

Wanted to be a Marine

I had a plan after high school.
I saw the future as the wizard, fixating

on the crystal ball, the size of a boulder. After graduating
high school, I was going to join the
few the proud: US Marine Corps—
then Pops bellowed in my face ferociously—
encouraging the erasure of my dream.

The breeze is letting go—when I walk out
onto the St. Mary's Park baseball diamond and look back:
a rustling leaf of the tree stops rustling,
a dream stops growing like a dead plant,

But I feel like a plane flying high, embarking on a new
manifestation   instead of combating my Salvadoran
and Nicaraguan cousins.

Penning Tonight

tonight, i pen the   melancholic lines
write, for instance, the night splintered
and the falling stars quiver from   afar
the night breeze swirls in the sky and chants
tonight, i pen the melancholic lines
            i adored her, and yesterday she loved me also
through nights like today, I embraced her tenderly
i caressed her often
she and I under the boundless   sky
                  Where she loved me and
somedays i loved her also and held   her huge quiet eyes

tonight, i can pen the melancholic verses
to know that I don't have her   to remember that she was disappeared
to discover this colossal night   still more colossal without her,
and the poem tumbles to the heart like rain to the meadow

i wish that she was here, so that I could see her

                  the night is broken, and she is not here

that's it! from afar, someone is chanting out of reach
my spirit shrieks and whimpers as i have lost her forever

Needed a Gun

I used to think it was harsh. In my old life,
some friends pierced their left ear
proving coolness, while others got
jumped into SF gangs
showing off their chingón side.

But these days, darker than night, not safe.

Gunshots reverberated hard
in empty night air, weakening my insides
as young boys expired
like fallings stars on
your blood-darkening sidewalks.

Stoned imagination
Scared
Trembling
I looked over my shoulder:

The same story. The same spooked heart.
Flickering fury, power needs, rather than a guitar:
hot firearms for sale
bought a thirty-eight special,
my fingers clenching it like a flower on top of Bernal Hill
as I stood near the children's laughter but never fired a gun.

The Hardened Heart

When Rudolfo's coffin descended into the earth, he reached the end.
His coffin rocked into the ground like a buoy or boat.

I would take my *corazón*, he said, and gift it to the campesino,
and they would slice it up and hand it back:

You can't ingest a heart within the four unlit
chambers where a human is detained indefinitely.

An adolescent soldier in the scorching sun, like an artist,
sculpts the face off the dead man with his knife.

And he dangles it on the mango tree, blossoms
along with the other like faces.

The *heart* is the hardest part of the body.
Sensitivity is in the lips.

The Rhythm of Revolution:
1979-1981

Never have you seen Nicaraguans
so alive: men and women dressed
in green, black, and red bandannas
danced collectively to the rhythms
of music blasting beats from radios
on every Managuan street corner and
flowed with melody and listen as the
voice within said, "I can dance, freely!"

The story goes: the Sandinista
People's Army established a new human pulse—
for the sake of literacy—the sowing of new seeds.
Body rediscovered. Root to Roots.
They were up to their hearts with
reading the written word:

El Campesino cracked codes, and the real revolution
began—
teaching Nicaraguans to read—young people trained,
like warriors of literacy, with uniforms and military—style battalions
and squadrons, uncorking light, fighting ignorance.

For hours el Campesino voraciously deciphered the
mysteries
of their finances and increased earning power,
women, like protagonists of their own bodies, exercised
control on the cycles of their bodies, reading birth
control literature.
For the Campaign, Nicaraguans aimed to fulfill
a fundamental promise: to show the younger generation
that solidarity and generosity, rather than weapons—
was the key to changing the country from age-old
backwardness.

At that time of the Revolution unfolding,
the new government smelled Uncle Sam's bad breath.
Was the turning over of weaponry enough? The
strength
of the Revolutionary story was built out of guerilla warfare,
moving a patriotic enterprise: The National Crusade for Literacy.

February 14, 1985

Beloved Ix Chel:

I am writing this short letter with intense emotions as we break from a dangerous guerrilla operation. Our mission was to hit and run, attacking an army battalion that surveils the mountain where our base is. After a long walk-through bombs and bullets, our group helped a wounded commander.

We descended the mountain and continued our journey to the capital, where the commander would receive medical treatment. We suffered no casualties, but the battalion had many: luck was on our side; and my compañera/os, and I are well prepared for guerrilla warfare.

But beloved Ix Chel, despite how difficult and precarious the war is, all things take on a feeling of faith when I think of our love, about the day we were introduced to each other, about the covert missions in which we fought side-by-side, about the sacred ritual when we chose our names Ix Chel and Pacal in memory of our Mayan ancestry, and swore our love to each other for eternity, and that juntos we would fight for social justice. We swore our love to each other for eternity and that juntos we would fight for social justice. And despite your absence, compañera, I continue to fight fearlessly, with dignity, and for Libertad!

I see the light of the mountain top and wonder where you are and what distance place you may be sleeping. And Ix Chel, I say to you that my heart still sees flashes and semblances of your departure so clearly in mind, the moment when we said, "love to eternity," the last warmth of your eyes seeing me, when you told me that "I Love you," your sad smile when you whispered to me, "Adios." But I find comfort in knowing that all this is just an anomaly in the endless path of our love.

Well, my beloved Ix Chel, the break is over, the people call, and the war continues. Nonetheless, the indestructible sun shines as our love continues. Please write me at the prearranged address.

"¡Contigo en lucha!"

Pacal

32

Yo Soy Amor/I am Love

I am Love like
Four falling stars in the day sky

That will speak a truth no one will chuckle at
My heart is sacred deep inside that is avid and awake

And burning

I am Love,
Whispering, "I love you! I love you!"
To the whole chaotic, crazy world

I have not won the battle against a world of enemies: A
nation of untruth has not relinquished my self-love

I am love/Amor:
A man awakes today with the ground to stand upon

And defend.

Run

Pretend a boom box
pops over your head. Run
fast, and cleats dig in the dirt. Run
as if scoring a touchdown. Look
to the left as if crossing
a crosswalk. Look to the right
as if the gang member is watching
you. Bend as if picking blueberries.
Do the pivot. Straighten up
as if you're military personnel.
Race do the race. Footwork
do the footwork. Do the arms
pumping—forward and backward.
Dig. Do the jump—jumping that
wall onto stairs. Your heart beats
frantically, all or nothing. Reach
and open the gate. Now, run. They're
shooting. Run fast and inhale.
Dive under the van, and don't

      Breathe.

Hands holding your face.
Drop down.
Face at the pavement.
Pray and pray.
Hear the gangsters run away.
Pray and pray.
Don't scream.

Remember

Remember the slip of the tongue that costs thousands
of deaths.
Remember seeing the pits where men and women were kept
for many days without food and agua.
Remember listening to the cocktail chat in which their freedom
hinged on.
Remember comprehending why men of good nature will read torture
reports with captivation.
Remember that such things as windmills and co-op farming
are insignificant and take a long-time.
Remember that Che Guevara is not here for this struggle and that Victor Jarra
was captured as others and assassinated.
Remember Jose Marti, nothing but landing strips in Cuba and Miami, while
there's no Malcolm X in the US professing revolution.
Remember trying on Gringos, your wordy and boring story of corruption. Still you
best give them what they desire:
Remember Lisa Alegro, who, after years of incarceration, did not know what day it
was how she walked with help and was required to crap in public?
Remember telling them about the razor, the electric wire, dry ice and concrete, gray rats,
and primarily who fucked her a multitude of times and when.
Remember telling them about revenge: Jose lying on the flatbed Toyota, motioning
his stumps in your face as his captors slashed off his hands.
Remember how they tossed his severed hands to the many acres of coffee, gone and silent,
and grip on the last chunks of leeched earth.
Remember to tell them Jose tried to sing in his last gasps of air and slashed hands
gripping the last chunks of leeched earth.

Remember that many weeks later, a labor leader was ripped into pieces and buried,
torn into pieces and buried.
Remember to tell them how his friends located the soldiers and forced them to dig him
up and ask for forgiveness of the corpse once it was pieced together like
a human.

No Tattoos

Every day there's the Bay Area, every day, every night, there's the gang, once, it
was you that they wanted as a member.

But I can't get tats. Pops warned me not to:
Tattoos are for criminals with life sentences that don't see the sun's golden glow
that nourishes the skin with vitamin D:

Besides, you are not a gangster:
Dangerous! Anxiety is amor's greatest killer, he said. Two years ago, in San Francisco,
every day and every night, there's Juno, whose tattoo was concealed under his
long sleeve shirt for protection.
Not safe having a tat: he was evading detection from rival gangs, like living in a
war zone, like
flirting with the devil, like hiding your subversive side in Central America.

A Prayer to La Virgen

I pray to you: Virgincita de Guadalupe
since you visited el Indio, Juan Diego,
after the wars, need protection for my family and friends in the US
and Central America,
secure for us with your utmost holy son
the benevolence of keeping our faith,
of cherished trust amid in malice of life,
of a blazing peace and charity,
bust open my chest like a jail cell
to let me out,
lovely mestiza virgencita
inspire my hoarse hair to spike up
over my heart like pine trees ablaze,
let me be your hijo and bestow
upon us with the beloved gift
of final perseverance.
Amen.

Outlawed

Hiding My Identity

¡Oye Cipote! I had to act Mexican to fit in
Mexico. I stitched up my new identity by
studying how a Chilango speaks: ¡No manches!
¡Hijole! ¡No hay bronca! ¡Esta chido, carnal!
I carried my Salvadoranness inwardly like a
masked man, acting Mexican, uttering
a language not mine surviving as a runaway
criminal not being noticed by the police: the
continuous subject to police harassment
and constant fear of being culturally outed
and deported.
In these truths, I find myself relieved, feigning
my identity that surfaces now.
My fear kept me from teaching others about
my past.

I don't blame myself.

41

Centro American?

¡Hey Ese! What is happening in Centro America is
in Los Estados, tambien. Checked it out, compa! Los Chicanos
have also been targets of systemic violence.

Have you heard of the Chicano Moratorium?
Here's how the historia goes, vato:

On August 29th, 1970, Chicanismo rose como tidal waves against
the establishment. A crowd: like a swarm of brown cockroaches,
attended the Chicano Moratorium antiwar protest, the largest
Mexican American protest to date.

But the chota stormed Laguna Park in Los Angeles. The LA Police
backed up by the Sherriff Department, bashed anyone's head in, gente
who looked or smelled brown like piñatas, ese!

The pigs attacked the peaceful rally like blood-thirsty Doberman pinschers,
injuring some, calling our gente dirty Mexicans, arresting many, and brutally
chilling-killing three Chicanitos!
One of those killed was Ruben Salazar, then the most chingón newspaper
journalist of Chicano background in the nation, worked several years
for the *LA Times* and at the time of the Moratorium worked
for KMEX as the Director.

Covering the Moratorium, Salazar and his news crew later went to the
bar—the Silver Dollar—to take a break during the riot. Without warning,
the Sheriffs appeared outside and shot three metal canisters into the bar.
One struck Ruben on the head, and he died in a flash of a breath.
Asi fue! Ruben targeted because he spoke out about police brutality!
And, some say, he was violently disappeared for reporting the Chicano
oppression en Los Angeles.
En Los United States, mi gente, in your country, it's illegal to be brown.
Pero Brown is beautiful! Brown is beautiful!

Know your history Indigena, know who you are, and know your roots!
They run deep and inside of you, tu essencia! You are more than Central American!

It's medicina for your alma.
Don't forget you were born in Los Estados Unidos!

The Guest

In soliloquy he whispers that el tiempo se acaba.
It is the sound of machetes cutting in cornhusks,

the hurt of some field music in Salvador.
The breeze along with the prison, heedful
as Ricardo's hands on the inside touch
the cold walls as he paces, it is his wife's voice

seeping into his cell each nightfall, and he
imagines her face to be his. It is a little country, and
there's no limit to the pain that men inflict onto others.

Cruising the Mission

Cruising the Mission in San Fran in the 72 gray Buick Skylark
 with my African American bruddas: Titus and Kenya
We kick it on a Wednesday afternoon & socializing, hanging out,
and traveling on wheels in the Mission District.
 Here the fast-food enterprise cashes in
on the spineless sale of Gringo and commercialized Mexican food like Taco Bell:
low-income Latinos are the bull's eye who buy tacos faster and cheaper.
The Taco wars are on against empty stomachs and pocketbooks.
Not wanting poisonous Tacos, we head to the Los Panchos restaurant.
We are hard-shelled bruddas and wouldn't get caught dead in a Taco Bell,
knowing what up with the Taco Bells and Jack-In-The Boxes.
Linked-in culture with
Rap music by
NWA's song- "Straight Out of Compton":

"You are about to witness the strength
 of street knowledge..."

The Kenwood stereo thumps
 where the other throbs.
Cruising the Mission, but lucky we're not high
 off a blunt or Old English
we're wide awake without light heads or blood-shot eyes
 rapping and singing in unison.

We become a quartet of hope and passion as if 1968
 we're loud in the warm company; people pass us
 with special songs.
The white cop senses us (the full feeling
as if by an obsession with historical distance, as if the dread
could not be pre-avoided--)
is that to be profiled, within his gaze, a fixed pattern—
stops the car in front of ours—
And the Five-0 gets out of his, buffed and pissed,
walks upon us with his 357 in hand like Dirty Harry—
Puta! —but this is not a movie--
he points the powerful piece onto Kenya's skull.

45

You read this history and may relate to it or not! Just beyond
this poem, words flow upstream.
But, the Cop, then, continues with his brutal ways and turns to all of us—
as if in terror mode—asking for our IDs.
As he walks back, the Cop says what we already know: we have clean records,
but warns that we should never follow
a cop as the switch could be turned off! Cruising the Mission! Our history is
meaningful and a hardened past.

US Immigration Law and Rulings

Naturalization Act of 1790, Naturalization Act of 1795, Naturalization Act (officially an Act to Establish a Uniform Rule of Naturalization; ch. 54, 1 Stat. 566), Alien Friends Act (officially An Act Concerning Aliens; ch. 58, 1 Stat. 570) Alien Enemies Act (officially An Act Respecting Alien Enemies; ch. 66, 1 Stat. 577), Naturalization Law of 1802, Naturalization Act of 1870, Page Act of 1875 (Sect. 141, 18 Stat. 477, 1873-March 1875), Chinese Exclusion Act of 1882, Alien Contract Labor Law (Sess. II Chap. 164; 23 Stat. 332, 1885), Immigration Act of 1891 Geary Act of 1892, United States v. Wong Kim Ark, 1885, Immigration Act of 1903 (Anarchist Exclusion Act), Naturalization Act of 1906, Immigration Act of 1907, Immigration Act of 1917 (Barred Zone Act), Immigration Act of 1918, Emergency Quota Act of 1921, Cable Act of 1922, Immigration Act of 1924 (Johnson-Reed Act), National Origins Formula of 1924, Mexican Repatriation Act of 1929, Equal Nationality Act of 1934, Nationality Act of 1940, Chinese Exclusion Repeal Act of 1943 (Magnuson Act), Immigration and Nationality Act of 1952 (McCarran-Walter Act), Operation Wetback, 1954, INA Amendments (Hart-Celler Act of 1965), Cuban Refugee Adjustment Act of 1966, Plyler v. Doe,[11] 457U.S. 202 (1982), Immigration Reform and Control Act of 1986, and the Immigration Act of 1990

Profiled

After the walking, after the talking,
the shopping--the challenge: most shopping outings
are exciting, adding to a bitty wardrobe.
To hear stories of criminality
is one thing. But to be viewed as a criminal
without just causes and adds emotional pain to the pain—
Black Security follows you around from aisle to aisle
like Inspector Gadget, thinking that you
are an infamous bank robber or shoplifter
from black or brown planet heathen.
What have you done for being profiled?
Punishment for being dark-skinned?
You fear being exposed to stressors stemming from racism.
You hope time works as a power wash,
cleansing the build-up to invisibility.
You wish you are evading that trend or even your butt
kicked by the Black Security Guard by walking in silence.
You're just shopping for new jeans!
You feel your color most when pushed
against that scathing white background.
Being of color cuts today!

Behind Supermax Walls

Underneath the smooth essence
of my eyes, deep and internal,
    A piece of me has expired.
I wipe my bloody hands
over it, brutal as an iron wall,
        Roam my fingers along   with it,
The cold-blue scars
Dam,   I AM TERRIFIED!
Terrified of what might become
        Of me, I, the authentic self
Behind these four corners.

Let Them Speak

Graffiti beauty & creation: large monuments of stone Silvio Orozco
sprays on about freedom. The Berlin walls splintered and fell.
And within Mexico's and US' silent histories, some chant quiet prayers

as Silvio Orozco sprays on about freedom.

For the thousands of vanished indigenous women--
disappeared while the cold winds blew north-to-south--
disappeared while the preying *machista* men murdered

like Champions of femicide! But Charles Bowden,
collector of violence against mujeres and niñas,
Like an artist for art's sake, won't

let them speak

of femicide. Look at his blurry, blurry writing and not hear the voices speak
of the disappearing brown women. Even as Bowden has passed, he relies on the

desert's shroud.

Yet, *agents of freedom* cruise helicopters, others
in military jeeps, robotic with pale faces lit
up by monitor screens, hunt for illegals on autumn
& summer days, etc.

In September, the susurrate leaves convert colors, glorifying
themselves in the dirt. Dinky white caskets waft down the trenches.
The stringy, frail branches become wise women who pray beside

one coffin, drops in the dirt road, drifting against palisades. Silvio
embraces himself on the dewy grass and smells its scent of melon, the ebony earth,
and the filtered, slight coolness of the wind.

He sprays on about Freedom on walls.

No one understands what he paints. The police identify him as subversive. The snobby, snooty people from the foothills disdain him, and the folks in Santa Fe are livid when they eye his black scribble on white walls.

Silvio renders the cosmic energy of his ancestors. He makes offerings around the mountain trails, amid poplars, esteeming respect.
But Enrique from Nicaragua gets what Silvio is saying.

But Carla from El Salvador sings the words to her children

after she buys frijoles from the mercado. Dario, el viejito,
el vecino who goes to see his sisters every other week in Juarez,
comprehends the graffiti.

In response to the whitewashed wall, the words project out through the paint
like detainees' fingers through prison bars
like loud gestures, gesturing at the toxic and malignant males

walking freely on the streets.

El Corralón

Hard not to speak up today, under the tides of detection—
migrants captured like one thousand thieves,

        silenced like dead voices, and uprooted
        history at various points along the border.

Five yellow buses screech to a halt on stolen ground.
Five yellow buses on rutted streets: full of undocumented

        persons bunched up like human cattle, then
        proceeding in a caravan to El Corralón:

No more giant INS detention center than El Corralón.
Like a nightmare, they reached their destination

        about 5 pm, nineteen hours after the
        initial detention proceedings.

Never will they forget this day; their dreams shattered
as glass confetti blown away by the wicked wind--

        now documented US criminals, photographed
        and forced to sign documents alien to their being.

Swallowed up by systemic quicksand, buried deep in it:

        men, women, and children from all over
        the world flock to the soccer field on prison grounds

where Mexicans--in large numbers--are detained.

Looking for a Reflection

Lost in Skin

It's hard for Willy right now—
not following the sure path of self,
projecting white supremacy on his strips
of brown skin as star constellations.

He's a wanderer from his identity
like misfortune
like the unthinkable,

his face, a semblance of Indigeneity; he can't pass as white.
Each day passes. One day after the other.
Their gone and never will come back but telling.

Willy's birthplace is only a blurring memory.
When will he go back to Nicaragua? When will he live again?

He dreams in the US, not set in the skin,
black and red Confederate flag posted on his gray bedroom wall.

Your Version of Jesus

Picture frame of Jesus, picture of blue-eyed white Jesus,
gone history silent; mouths full of rocks; wall spaces open,
still like a blank journal ready to speak.

You and your history paint a white background, framing Jesus
as another White Superhero or protagonist planted deep in your mind.
Do you feel comfortable saying this to me? Do you fear power loss?

The trees, the bark, leaves, also the dead ones are vibrant and wet.
Your version of your white Jesus is your version, taking off my glasses,
no longer blind like an impoverished student of history.

Oral history, my ancestors speak through me. We close in on your history
like deep water. As if a small pinch of turquoise dust is waiting on the other
side of my clear window, breathing and telling the brown/black version of Jesus.

You are breathing and saying that many churches in the world sketch Jesus as black
or brown. Orthodox Christians close the door to European art—if you enter
a church in Africa, you'll likely gaze at an African Jesus—who stares back at you!

Lost in Mirror

You start another day alone and forget.

Who you are; you drink the last

guzzle of foamy beer from the pint glass

beside strangers, telling yourself

that you will stop drinking.

But the temptation is too great!

In San Francisco, bars and liquor stores

are ubiquitous like the ocean water.

You drive alone on the wet pavement wonder

what color the sky is in the US.

Does the world today have open spaces?

Doors, or windows? Looking into the mirror,

you find in the junkyard four walls close in.

You can never find yourself lost.

So, you open the fridge again, snap open a cold

cerveza and feel piercing pain below your right rib cage.

Nothing changes; life goes on.

Prima Lucia

I don't see the world that prima Lucia
sees when she talks about Nicoya politics—
crazy conservative talk of Somoscismo--
the blind babble of a democracy.
Hard to talk to her! Lucia forgets Somoza
is one of the bloodiest dictatorships in history.

Lucia and I don't see eye to eye.
But she's familia and blood is thicker
than water, my sister reminds me.
I want to accept her as a friend.
I want to accept her for who she is.

When Lucia talks Somoscismo, my heart
hurts as my blood pressure spikes up.
She closes her ears when I remind her
that Somoza ripped off Nicaragua's US
earthquake aid like the thief he is:

without any heart for the poor and hungry.
What she thinks, what humanity means to
her, will never go away—only our bond as
family matters, I guess.

Realidad/Reality

Lechita blanca
Y canela negrita
heirbe tan calientito.

Vuela El Cuervo negro
free in the blue sky:
Circles White
Mountain.

Olas are
Bluegreen
Sol y arena, brown
Owl
fixated on
agua.

Little boy looks at mirror
Closes eyes and
sees dots.
Reflection black silhouette. El Palo verde:

The wind fierce and leaves
shiver. La ojita falls on soil.

Niña Carlotta

La Niña Carlotta, who lives in San Salvador in the small
blue house: bluer than the heavens above, frowns upon
her broken flowers. At 65, her Mayan-dark skin
is darker today, enough that her moon doesn't smile
nor glow.

We set the goals with four square bricks, solid enough
to mark both goals and bright enough to see where I will kick
el balón, and score a gol like los estrellas: Pelé o Maradona,
the best strikers in the history of el fútbol Americano.

Niña Carlotta's spirit shattered into 1 million pieces —
as she retrieves our balón and assaults its hard grain
leather with her silver hunting knife--piercing, puncturing,
killing our field of dreams.

The ball slowly hissed--flattened--air spills out.

Abuelitas

Abuelita Rafaela and Maria look india,
but no one talks about it!

Abuela Rafaela wears her hair only in a bun.
Once I saw her hair down when I pretended to snore.
Abuelita, Pop's mother hella resembles him to the T!

Abuela Maria's olive-brown skin, much darker
than Mom's who looks española y güera.

Abuelita Rafaela hums hymns in Spanish under her breath.
Abuela Rafaela should have been a gardener, wearing
San Francisco's daylight on her face while watering the garden.

Abuelita Maria never smiles, wearing resentment, knowing betrayal.
Abuela Maria, married to Abuelo Pablo in Nahuizalco, at fourteen,
her home scriptures, stolen, lost her home, left in the needy,
bearer of 11 children, depressed when Abuelo died.

Abuelita Rafaela and Maria, both from Central America,
both look india, visiting San Francisco.

Time circles around them
in an alien world. I wonder
and wait to get to know them.

Triple Cords

Evening, and I walk past the man-made park
where the gray pigeons peck for pan on pavement—
I am concerned from head to toe—the light in
my mind weakens and flutters out of whack,
not academically sound.   I feel scared, shielded
from pain part of my existence--receiver of belt lashes

unleashed by pissed-off Papa, a listener not but a hitter first.
Master planning as I wear three pairs of Cords,
anticipating getting fired on by belt lashes.

Under suspicion, I am for a red-inked report card.
Under stress, while wearing three pairs of cords

for shielding against the lashes, I need this plan.

How strong am I?

Want to Sing

I shake like a frozen leaf
shaking and afraid to ask for help after the snow.
My heart breaks into pieces: shards of glass on the cement pavement,
lost my song to sing, staying silent and mute,
                    misaligned from my emotions, can't speak my truth.

Who am I? What door am I going to kick down to sing again?
                    I want to reach the stars to speak to my ancestors.
I keep banging the heavens when it's dark
with my Sawed-off shotgun dream. Someday I'll hit
   it big!
                    Peeling off my senses from my bare bones, blasting the moon
   wide open:
just fixated there will be liberation.

Deafening Voices

Mom's Voice

¡Hijo! Mom said.
I only loved to go out dancing
once a week many years ago
in Sonsonate, El Salvador.

             --a storytelling, ceaseless
                     voice—

But my mother called me chispita: the little spark
of a woman that danced but those men would leer at.

                     --a quivering, fiery
                         voice—

¡Hijo! Mamma Rosa utters.
Your Abuela Marita feared
my innocence would have been taken:
The Salvadoran military, the violator.

                  --a protesting
                    voice—

El Salvador was never the same.
Historia states that during the 1932 Matanzas:
the Military restored order in a brutal way.

                   --a recollecting,
                     gesturing
                     voice—

And I migrated to California.
In San Francisco, I danced again:
safely and freely as an uncaged bird.
Hopefully, I will return to live in my pais,
my homeland when it is safe!

                  --a longing, whispering
                     hopeful
                     voice.

Cry Baby

Papi is crying like a chillón, tears spilling
down his face as the muscles of his chin, tremble.
Men and boys don't cry? lashes heavy with tears,
brick by brick, his walls come tumbling down.
Wailing and suffering, his sobs echoed in the empty house.
I watch and witness Papi's secret tears. Flood gates
open. He told me once: that men don't cry.
Broken-hearted. Tightened chest. Papi's mirror:
I am. I hold in my rain showers. Pops riddled
stomach: gastric acid stress. Nicaraguan, he is.
Fled his homeland and diseased with poverty,
he arrived in San Francisco, and there worked a trade.
Disabled he became. Now Papi earns SS benefits.
Poor again! pinching pennies to feed us.
My eyes drip with tears. I can't stop crying!

Can Speak English

My 2nd week of high school at ISA was historical.
I was born a US Citizen and am proud of it. You see!
My parents, Central Americans, spoke to me
in Spanish at home and learned English like a champ
at St. Charles School in the heart of the Mission.
Privileged as a Latino but blessed to be bilingual:
I speak English as I read the dry classics like Romeo and Juliet.
I speak Spanish as I sing and dance to Tito Puente's lyrics.
But, today, Mr. Richardson, my English Substitute teacher,
as sharp as a bowl of Jell-O, asked if I
speak English. American like you: fuck'n White dude!
I reply as silence can't protect me as I am pissed.
After the offending, after the cussing, he kicked me out of class,
kicked out for being insulted as I was offended!
What I trip, I don't feel safe in school.

The Gray-Haired Black Man

The day I stood up to the brown lady, the SF Muni bus was blowing cold air, not dense with people, not crowded like yesterday.

There were no singing children or adults, not even a crying baby, this morning. Only the gray-haired African American man, the middle-aged lady with the black sweater rode the bus on this day. And my viewpoint projected from the back corner of the bus.

I didn't like being in a weak seat where someone I couldn't see could see me. The back Seats are my favorite seats. The back was hollow. The back was empty.

So, on this day, my silence was like a painter's canvass without the paint. I had been holding back my anger, frustration, never talking back to my screaming parents. My high school English class was boring, and I didn't like reading Shakespeare!

But, on this day, when the middle-aged brown lady with the black sweater started mouthing off to the gray-haired African American man as she stared down at him, chirping that black people are too loud and kept complaining about being oppressed.

But when she called him a black monkey that needs to go back from where he came from: something told me that enough is enough! My history is his historia. My skin is dark. His skin is dark too. Her stupid words stung like a bumblebee.

Like the brave Muhammad Ali, I got up from my seat and walked up on the brown woman and bellowed loudly like a dragon from the top of my lungs: leave him alone, he's family! I said.

The woman, who I know was Latina, then looked at me with her bulging green eyes, and retreated to the back of the bus, running scared, as the bus road away into fog-laced air.

I asked the gray-haired African American man if he was okay. He smiled with his sweaty face persisting and brought his right hand to his chin. Then he slowly pulled it away, signing words, thinking he was saying thanks.

I sigh as I felt relief in my head and stomach and took the empty seat next to him. My desire to speak out loud was now limitless as a lake.

Taking Your Jobs?

In the grape fields working at hot depths: the
scorching sun burns away—boleros blur my mind

to distract from the sea of grapes. Pruned and reaped
vines tied and ready, rough dia more to prune and cut,

then, jolted by the Salinas' 95-degree heat, t-shirt soaked
and wet, desperately trying to focus on the damp vines.

Days routine between day and night until you sleep
four-to-five hours when resting unsoundly.

Weeks of remembering erroneous gringo chisme:
that the farmworker is stealing jobs is cold!

You don't have the backbone to work in burning heat.
You don't want to expose your lungs to pesticides.

The life of a farmworker is like a specter—he isn't essential
to people--the machinery of growers has more value.

Last week, a Nicaraguan friend collapsed as a choking
and girdling tree died of heat exhaustion.

The nearest water cooler was a ten-minute walk away.
The foreman is so strict that he doesn't allow breaks.

But he wouldn't take a machine to the field without
putting oil in it, but a life taken away, stripped of basics to live.

You wouldn't want to be in our place; you wouldn't be seen.
So how can you say that we are ripping off jobs?

Walk the rows like a tired child unable to stop.
Up at dawn readying to work the fields with my hands.

The long days of swivel of wrist to snip fruit.
The heavy arms and sweaty smell.
The cases filled with fruit, not taking jobs!

Tongue Split

My tongue is split in two by

benefit, fortune, and destiny

words flow out of my mouth
standing on each other

relishing being a voice:

conveying anticipating inferences
My tongue is split in two

into deep cadences fragments of daze

into splendor or mishap

uttering words that cut the heart
My tongue split by power

by our foolish hunger to succeed or conquer

My tongue split into matching parts
one yearns to swear and hum boisterously

the other one desires to inquire for peace

My tongue split in two
one side enjoys celebrating

the other one chooses to go into recluse to ruminate

tongue

español of the melodic sounds

tongue

the flowy sounds in english

tongue

spanish of 5 vowel sounds

tongue

14 vowel sounds in ingles

tongue

español of nasal sounds

My tongue occasionally behaves like binaries

and goes berserk
not grasping which one ought to be talking

which one paraphrasing

My tongue split into two
US Customs barges in the center

questioning my words

asking for my California ID
asking for me to speak Ingles

My tongue split into two

My tongue split into two

I love my tongue
it utters and aligns with truth

I love my tongue: It utters and aligns with truth

Lost in Translation

Latino/Central American, I am with my California
ID and English words flowing so smoothly

like the true American that I am who was born freely
on US soil to Spanish-Speaking parents were not
fluent speakers of the English language. At times they
both got lost in translation as lost as two ants

who would try to cross the highway during rush hour?
while sis, bro, and I conversed in English during the times
that we would complete our English homework.

Hopeless to Displace Them

The poor are countless,
and true,
it's useless to ignore them
Really,
at sunrise,
they spot
the Transamerica Building
where they'd
like to live with their niños
They can
bear on their shoulders
the coffin of the celestial
They can
ruin the air like rabid birds
to a black eye, the sun

But unclear of the jewelry
        they stop and go through the mirrors of
                    bruises
The poor
wander and die slowly

That's why
It's hopeless to displace them

Healing Fault Lines

Write Your Story

You know the voice of depression
    Still shouts to you

You know those habits can injure your life
    Still, write your story

But you are a man and not emotionally tuned
    Still project mourning onto paper

Your human, so permit yourself permission to cry out
    And even bloom

    Keep squeezing word drops from the Sun
From your silence and translate into a new tongue
And from under your grief runs joy with silken words

    Keep squeezing word drops from the Sun
From the precious voice comes recovery of Spirit

    And your dear,
From not having much knowledge yet in grief
    make your words fierce

Learning to recognize that putting words to the pain
Is a wealth of a joyful heart rhythmically fusing?
    But linguistically and revelatory,

    Like an Unbroken man,
Behind your writing comes relief.

Poem Offering

I write this poem for you
since I am tired and losing hope.
Hug it like a soft teddy bear
when it rains; it will cover you,
wear it like a winter coat

        the snow will not sting through,
                te quiero

I have not much energy nor money
so, it's a warm pot of gallo pinto
to fill your tummy during an economic
depression
it's a sun visor for your head, to wear

        over your face, to protect your skin
                te quiero

Hold it, esteem it as your reflection
when you are uprooted, needing grounding--
the garden loves ample compost & soil
And in the side of the chest box in your closet
hidden away like a hut or a shack
in the dense Redwoods, visit,

        I will speak to you with compassion & care
                te quiero

It's all I have to gift
all you need to do is palpitate and open
and to go on flourishing internally
when the power policies reconstruct
your invisibility, and illegal status

        Recollect and don't forget
                te quiero

How to Make Pupusas

Tip the sun into the bowl so you can honor and remember your Mayan ancestors who never faded away or disappeared like the mist in the morning? You fill it with 1 cup of vegetable oil, corn masa flour, 3 lbs. of graded Monterey Queso, and 1 cup of water, mixing it in. You start kneading the masa as Mamá does it with her soft-smooth hands that have gently rubbed your forehead to rub away your migraine headaches. She rolls the masa into balls, makes an indentation with her right thumb, and fills it with the cheese or other ingredients (I love the combination of cheese with loroco, the herbaceous flower bud). With Mamá's therapeutic hands, she pats it into a round tortilla. Then she grills the pupusa on the comal until it browns on both sides.

Eat the hardened rainbow with your crimson sky mouth and celebrate Easter Sunday. Hide the milk-chocolate Easter bunnies behind the blueberry bushes that stand tall above the cheery children and serve the pupusas with Horchata and a plate of rice and beans.

Since Dad and Mom are laid off--don't worry--pupusas are on the cheap to make. Dance Cumbia and Salsa and make more pupusas. Party time!

The Field

This is a field where war is nonexistent,
becomes as calm as the rushing waves of the ocean.
We live in one world:
a habitat without hornet nests where the brown, black, white, or yellow soldier

does not perish or be praised for heroics in the name of God.
This is a field where raindrops, drop—
one drop after the other—it's all water,
from the heavens above,
all abundant, food for all, no more Monsanto.

This is a field were physical or mental
borders do not inspire hate: acts of betrayal to the heart.

This is a field where children run freely in the streets, not fighting for freedom,
nor dodging the holy bullet from the freedom fighter, no need for revolution.

It's the exemplar world—
a full-hearted world,
a dream you dream together is real.

This is a field like no other:
It's genuinely an equal-playing field without human depreciation
and unconditional love isn't blurred by academic philosophies.

Leaning on Love

Leaning into the day in San Francisco, we walk into each other's lives
like magic beneath an unveiled sun as our diasporas interlock.

While God sent out the red signals across our full eyes, we gaze
at each other as if we'd be happy to stare forever.

Our hearts reflect the ocean waves or deep mirrors of yellow stars.
Our hearts project onto each other, our hidden flame.

As we both flutter internally, we see the springing wild seed
blown along the road by the wild wind.

The heavens unfastened: opening a clear pool where no hate or war
can dare to swim and its depth everlasting.

We smile—capturing sunshine onto our faces—the world a better place.
Our souls crack open as we hear the song of endless sea music.

We dance for hours and do not stop, feeling desire in our glorious art,
carving a space in our rose garden, flashes and foreshadows of love.

Leaning onto the present, we have become each other's complete mirror.
We are a couple now and drink the red wine on our divine table.

Now we embrace each other in holy matrimony—as intertwined as threads
of yarn—we have become one with each other, burning in the same flame.

The truth has been divinely conceived: our union is like the Redwood tree,
rooted into the earth for eternity.

We hold each other's hands, never letting go: our fire keeps burning, and

left behind our Central America where the beggar picks through the garbage

looking for a living.

Bilingual Love

Bilingual, I am a recipient of two tongues:
Spanish and English, uttering words like the
Chameleon switches from one color to other
colors. My identity shifts and in transition—
code-switching from Español to English--gifted
by Central American migrant parents. They
sowed the seeds of power on the other side
of the border, a proliferation of fertile
American spaces for singing songs. Open
borders wide open to gift the sweet-hearted spirit with
the words of Bilingual Love--a synergistic celebration--
a transcultural world in transition as history
is told simultaneously in ingles and Spanish.

Let's sing and dance together to the powerful
sounds of the rhythm of language--
    lyrical music: Bilingual Love.

Baseball=Life

I smell the fresh-cut grass of the ballyard:
My six or seven senses are alive like a dream.
Running to the left as the loud Baseball is
belted by the bat, and I snag it at shortstop
like Ernie Banks as it snaps my Wilson glove.
Then I throw off my left foot to first, and barely
throwing out fast Racer.
Life and Baseball are nearly the same things.
Pops taught me: live life one day at a time--
and forget the past, the Present coveted.
Life is about not sweating the small things.
Baseball is about fundamentals, period!
You stay humble, courageous, and fearless.
You stay confident--cool--not arrogant.
¡Béisbol es vida…mil gracias Papa!

Canto

Te canto una canción; es mi deseo.

El viento es fuerte y el Árbol siente su fuerza.

Pero, esta canción la canto durante la guerra.

Te canto una canción, pero se va con el viento.

Te canto esta canción como le canto a las estrellas.

Vives en El Norte, como la luz del sol que brilla.

Sing

I sing you a song; it's my desire.

The wind is strong, and the tree feels its

strength. But I sing you this song during the

war. I sing you a song. But it goes with the

wind. I sing you this song like I sing to the

stars. You live in the North like the sunlight

that shines.

Luz (light)

La luz penetra el árbol y el viento se va.

Y regresa como la lluvia que moja las hojitas

verdes de a hora, pero para y regresa mañana

o en dos días. La luz que brilla en tus ojos,

brilla en los míos. También, por favor traigas tu

corazón cerca de mí. Solo me importa

satisfacer tu apetito con libertad. Tararcas

tonos juguetones de música y preocúpate para

dar amor.

Light (luz)

The light penetrates the tree and wind leaves.

The light returns like the rain that wets the green

leaves today but stops and returns tomorrow

or in two days. The light that shines in your

eyes shine in mine; please bring your heart near me.

All I care about is sufficing your appetite with freedom.

Hum playful tones of music and care about giving love.

Holding the Hummingbird

To Love, I am on the path
that I never thought of.
Now that I see the reflection
you have gifted me with,
I scream and shout as I feel the
piercing pincers in my heart.
I/me dream of being free
to embracing the potential
of whom I want to be.
The Hummingbird that I hold
with my worn and rough hands
but maternally and softly as it desires.
Now I know that I earned my wings.
It's time for me to soar.
As it buzzes away, my memory
reactivates self-discovery.
I/me see the path to self-expression:
keen awareness to always seek
the sweetness nectar.
I will reach the heights within me,
not forgetting the birth of Madre Earth's
first sunflower.

Nature the Heart

It is time to be quiet and
calm as the ocean breeze
cools and nurtures the spirit.

Nurture the breath and
think good thoughts as you
rest the delicate heartstrings,
no different than the water that
nourishes and permeates the
roots of the Aloe Vera plant.

Nurture the use of your words
and utter them as you think
with your mind rather than with
your heart.

Nurture the mind; it's time for
self-care: a gift to embrace,
reinvigorating your energy with
Self-Love.

Then, you Nurture the Collective:
The global community deserves your self-nurturance
while the upsurge for promoting freedom and
equality grows stronger than yesterday.

Stop Silence

When your father screams at you, tell him: Papi, don't scream. Words puncture the heart, letting the air out and flattening your balloon.

When the teacher teases and shames you for wearing your starch-creased Ben Davis khakis, do not cower. Then look him in his bulging beady-blue eyes, to fire back, to tell him not to

be afraid of his white reflection: racism is his strange fruit with blood on the leaves and blood-stained at the root; his soul's burden.

When you learn all the lines for the Christmas play, fly like the Eagle above the cumulus clouds because you can do it.

When Louie, Louie invites you to smoke heroin, tell him that you don't want to wake up under a cypress while you listen to the crickets sing to the rhythm of frigid wind.

Do not be afraid to hug your half-brother, who looks like your twin, looking in your mirrors.

When African Americans men shoot at you in that 66 Malibu Chevelle and are not blasted, pray to tell your God one million thanks as you kiss the solid ground you stand on.

When the boy with the meddling shadow says he's ugly like Caliban, do not walk away. Say:

Do not question that you're beautiful!

When your uncle says you run heavy-footed rounding the bases, please take it as constructive criticism.

Set the timer to run suicides. Run the bleachers. Don't miss baseball practice.

When the next friend asks you why you let your hair grow long, smile, then ask why have you cut yours so short?

When your father screams at you, tell him: Papi, don't scream! Words puncture the heart, letting the air out and flattening your balloon.

When your friend wants you to go to movies to see the *Romero* film, tell her that you are too young and that images of war cause secondary trauma.

When your mother says that she won't talk to you because she's mad, tell her you loathe the tumor. This dusk frazzles you like a curse.

When you discover that your cousin can't speak English, please don't laugh at her. Then help her with the English homework.

When you find out that you have the same ancestors, be proud. Then help her with the English reading.

Don't cover your face when you cry in front of your brother because he learned that Dad is cheating on Mama; your eyes are a fountain the thirsty crave. Flow into him.

When your father screams at you, tell him, Papi, don't yell. Words puncture the heart, letting the air out and flattening your balloon.

When you see your Mama frown, kiss her on the forehead and thank her for birthing you.

You are Jesus. He is who heals. Miracles cannot be counted.

When the older man with gray hair and rotten teeth calls you a spic and a nigger. Flick him the finger. Give him Bob Marley's "One Love/People Get Ready." Give him the palabra de Dios.

When your so-called next-door neighbor calls the migra on your primo, remind him that he's a border crosser too.

When your so-called best friend caps on JR and calls him a fat brown bitch, tell him to stop because words burn the skin.

This is Apocalypse, reclaiming what the dark side has stolen.

Do not fear. Do not wince. Do not inquire.

When your father screams at you, say no more and revive.

Your silence turned atomic. And it's a vacuum, speak up!

See What I See

See through the multitude of Redwood, Eucalyptus, and Oak Trees, which encircle
the light.

Remember the blueness of the clear sky.

The way fog lingers in the air but burns away.

Gather your eyes, and windows to your soul, the sky looks clearly like the ocean as it
extends no matter where you live on Earth.

See what I see: the same sky, drenched in golden light, never slipping through
my fingers.

I am alive to see the marvels of Mother Earth, brown
                                    like the color of my skin.

Jan 20, 1981

I Am President!

I am the President of the United States of America!
I call for the redistribution of Wealth: United we stand,
underneath the Red, White, and Blue.

I am the President of the United States! I have eliminated
poverty: Filet Mignon, water, Kale salads, frijoles, and bread
for every human being; God Bless America! United we are
like the Bald Eagle circling in the blue sky, *sweeping
our hearts clean with sacred wings.*

I am the President of the United States! The White House is
no longer white. But we painted it with multilayer of colors.
Yes, we are now truly the United States of America, seeing each
other: eye-to-eye. God Bless America! We are the land of the free!

Essence

it is a matter of essence,
of unspoiled tears   of being side-stepped on,

and forever, forever
seeing the humanizing   heart
peer deep to find the dabs
of hope and spirt,

so spit bars hermanos y hermanas,
so, sing   the morning star will
remember   your cumpleaños behind
humiliation   the new spring seedlings
like flaming sprouts   will hold you,

as you start every new year

You are essence--my brothers!
You are essence--my sisters!

Madre Seed

Five hundred years and   counting
tortillas shaping   between my sisters' hands,
grandmothers let the mountains speak to them,
and the corn stalks,
standing erect and grounded, braiding   interlocking
four roots into one   ever empowering
Madre-seed
bridge piecing together   the four directions,
blood boomeranging
in several directions,
connecting the south to north,   east to west

Five hundred years and   counting
writing history and prayers come   forth,
arms interlocked with other arms--Alianza,
keeping the force firm,
unsevered trust, sage faith
from Pipiles,   Janaab Pakal I,   Sandino and Oscar Romero,
to the silent men & women pacing on street corners
meditating on the horizon,
to the woman kneeling on cathedral   pews to reciting hymns
in the light of morning,
to purring, newborn   infants
being born and   a full moon shining

Five hundred years and   counting
and still existing and living
all shining and beating with seeing hearts,
tenacious
hearts singing   and fluttering dancing
acts of fortitude   flower shower
with virtue
that beams on
               our cell memory

Safe House

my aunts, uncles, and cousins escaped war
from Central America,
where dreams burned to ashes as
hot rocks cool after a summer rain.

It happens that our house of hearts,
in San Francisco, a sanctuary
 a respite,
doors opened outstretched like hands,
transforming their suffering into songs of
  celebration,
welcoming their boundless desires of
  being.

You see, they are from my same tree--
  welcome family--
even though my seed sprung on US soil,
an offspring of Central American parents--
  welcome family--
strengthening their convictions to
  breathe lightly.

my aunts, uncles, and cousins now live
  in our safe house,
no longer worried about their bedroom
floor shivering as they trembled
  to pray,
no more death squads pounding their
  doors,
picking at them with their metallic beaks.

Our house, with my massive soul,
  it reopens their hearts
where fire flickers and laughter swirls.
my aunts, uncles, and cousins,

stopped being
endless nights, a discarded book no one read,
   remembering youthful pleasure,
giving off light in their new home.

Mestizo

        my identity
              is not fixed,
                    but fluid

here is
the African
within me

who prays
one-to-three
        times a   day.

Behind
      my
soul

      there is
a Moor
      smiling

my eyes
      still gaze

at   Andalucía

But my
    mouth is
      Maya

       My dark
hands are
Pipil

My cheekbones
      fiercely as
      Sitting Bull's

My mind
perceives
      no borders

      no hegemony
no laws
no rulers

for this
      vagabond's
heart

Gratitude

To my FLOWERSONG PRESS community, especially Edward Vidaurre

To my support network, community, and friends at Creative Sonoma, especially Kirsten Madsen, Debra Yarro, and Bernadette Marko

&

Doing powerful work: Raizes Collective, The Parking Lot Poets, The California Poets in Schools, Arelene Francis Center, Burbank Housing, Latino Service Providers, Los Cien, Center for Wellbeing, North Bay Organizing Project, Sonoma County Organization: LandPaths, and The Sonoma County Poet Laureate Selection Committee.

In appreciation: Professor Melissa Moreno, Professor Andrew Jolivette, Dr. Tony Jimenez, Professor Iris Dunkel, Professor Nancy Mirabel, Professor Michael Hames-Garcia, Professor Norma Klahn, Professor Lynn Stephen, Professor Carlos Aguirre, Professor David Vasquez, Chad Bolla, Maria Freebairn-Smith, Thomas Hickey, Joaquin Lopez, Will Kenya Pearson, Miguel Rivera, Johnny Alfaro, Maria Canas, Amanda Ayala, Isabel Lopez, Martin Zuniga, Philip Mancus, Michael Gois, Paco Cano, Yancey, and Kevin Quiñones, Jay Gaynor, Carlos Lopez, Matt Sedillo, Dan Schurman, Kristy Gray, Bethany Facendini, Eric Boehm, Roselee Cabrera, Douglas Calderon, Frank Valerio, Aldaberto Aparicio, and Tim, and Jill Barger.

Special thanks to Black Freighter Press, especially Tongo Eisen-Martin, The Latin American Latino Studies Department at UC Santa Cruz, The Ethnic Studies Department at San Francisco State, The Ethnic Studies, Latin American Studies, and Comparative Literature Departments at the University of Oregon, the Woodland Community College, San Jose City College, and Hartnell College.

Mucho agradecimiento y amor para: Mi mama Rosa L. Garay, y papa Ernesto M. Garay, la madre de mi hijo Korina Campos, mi hijo Pakal, mi hermana, mi hermano, mis primos, primas, tíos, y todas las amistades que han tocado mi corazón.

Acknowledgements

Alarcón X., Francisco. *Borderless Butterflies: Earth Haikus and Other Poems*. Lake Isabella, CA: Poetic Matrix Press, 2014.

Alarcón X., Francisco. *Snake Poems: An Aztec Invocation*. San Francisco, CA: Chronicle Books, 1992.

Anzaldua, Gloria. *Borderlands/The New Frontera*: The New Mestiza. Aunt Lute Books, 1987.

Avilés, Quique. "My Tongue is Divided in Two." *Poetry Foundation,* 4 May 2018, https://www.poetryfoundation.org/poems/53006/-my-tongue-is-divided-into-two.

Baca Santiago, Jimmy. Healing Earthquakes. New York: Grove Press, 1952.

Baca Santiago, Jimmy. Singing at the Gates. New York: Grove Press, 2014.

Bencastro, Mario. *Odyssey to the North*. Houston, Texas: Art Público Press, 1998.

Dunkle, Jamahl, Iris. *Gold Passage*. Tennessee: Trio House Press, 2013.

Dunkle, Jamahl, Iris. *There's A Ghost in this Machine of Air*. Cincinnati, OH; WorldTech Editions, 2016.

Forsche, Carolyn. *The Country Between*. US. New York: Copper Canyon Press, 1981.

Galeano, Eduardo. *Memoria del fuego I. Los nacimientos*. México DF: siglo veintiuno editores, s.a.,1982.

Harjo, Joy. "Eagle Poem." *Poetry Foundation,* 2 January 2019, https://www.poetryfoundation.org/poems/46545/eagle-poem.

Herrera, Felipe, Juan. *Jabber-Walking*. Sommerville, Massachusetts: Candlewick Press, 2018.

Hillman, Brenda. *Practical Water*. Middletown, CT: Wesleyan University Press, 2009.

Murgia, Alejandro, and Paschke, Barabara, eds. *Volcán: Poems from El Salvador, Guatemala, Honduras, and Nicaragua*: San Francisco: City Lights Books, 1983.

Rumi, Muhamad., Jalal ad-Din. *Love's Ripening: Rumi on the Heart's Journey*. Boston & London: Shambhala Publications, Inc., 2010.

Zamora, Javier. *Unaccompanied*. Port Townsend, Washington: Cooper Canyon Press, 2017.

About The Author

Ernesto M. Garay's writings have appeared in the *DI-VêrRSé-City Anthology 2020, Redwood Writers 2016 Poetry Anthology, Pterodáctilo, and Ethnic Studies Journal.* Garay is the author of one collection of poetry: *Reverberating Voices.* He is *LA Revista Bilingüe: La Voz's* Person of the Month in Sonoma County for March 2020, a 2019-2020 Sonoma County, California, Discovered Award Recipient in Literary Arts, and an Ethnic Studies Associate Faculty at San Jose City College, Woodland Community College, and Hartnell College. Garay now lives in San Francisco and Sonoma County with Pakal, his son.

Printed in the USA
CPSIA information can be obtained
at www.ICGtesting.com
LVHW031539150823
755263LV00003B/175

9 781953 447616